My Bother Whose Art Is Heaven

Tom E. Jandric

Cover illustration by: Rosemary Ruffenach.

ISBN 13: 978-1-64343-593-0
Library of Congress Catalog Number: 2023921589
Printed in the United States of America
First Printing: 2023
27 26 25 24 23   5 4 3 2 1

Book design and typesetting by Pat Maloney.
Set in Adobe Song.

Legacy Pond Press
939 Seventh Street West
Saint Paul, MN 55102
(952) 829-8818
www.BeaversPondPress.com

I'd like to dedicate this book to my lovely daughter,
Great Kate of the lake.

Contents

Triton's Revenge

Mammals left the ocean, searching
for food.   Maybe . . .   Maybe,
the grass was greener.   Maybe,
that cold clammy feeling
got old?

Dry, warm beaches proved . . . penetrable.

Smells . . . an unexpected addition.
Breathing at will . . . a fringe benefit.
Sex on the beach . . . timeless.
Birthing . . . a blessing.
Life in the tropics . . . paradise.

Adaptations proved helpful.
Growing hair . . . much warmer.
Ditching the fins . . . better transport.
Opposing thumbs . . . grasping reality.
Phalanges . . . counting blessings.

Evolution's revolving door,
shuts some species out; while
others transition.

Fish fly,
birds swim;
unlike the platypus, who
just couldn't decide.
(Jealous seal and walrus cousins may join us later.)

Science explains why saltwater is undrinkable.
In truth, Triton feels the rejection . . . curses us.
Now, returning is impossible.

Preparing for Timelessness

Alzheimer's breaks time's bullying bondage.
Streetcars take them to a mystical land,
where memories assume precedence, derailing time's chronology.
Pushing aside reality (forgetting the now),
they are unbounded by consequences.

Memories act as foxholes.
Stumbling into well-worn trenches,
their stories revive themselves from a
labyrinth of their recollections.

Normally people open their biography to
some chapter that graciously welcomes them back.
Now memories have no table of contents.
The internal clock never gets rewound.
Their chronological lines of longitude
are not in sync with the Greenwich meridian.

Alzheimer's prepares them for the afterlife,
by being in sync with the timelessness of it all.

Infinite Possibilities

During times of conviction,
uncertainty is elusive.
Alternatives go unheeded.

When obscurity triumphs,
desperate searching for light scours the shadows.

Starlight can only be seen in darkness,
yet is constantly present.
Always revealing a vast universe of possibilities.

Ruminating on the Dock

Nature's matchmaker introduces hydrogen and oxygen.
Water becomes Earth's legal tender.
Mothering all elements in a global terrarium, like a petri dish,
it becomes the perfect porridge
(the embodiment of Goldilocks' obsession).

Water storms all fortresses of matter, like marauding medieval armies.
This Trojan horse constantly penetrates our epidermal layer.
Wrinkled bathtub toes defend my position.

Rivers are entrance ramps to the sea, constantly desiring to chauffeur all things back
to Eden
(before the sapiens invasion).

Dangling my feet,
in soft encompassing water;
stirrups a veil surrounding them.

A curious sunfish bites my toe.
Their investigating mouths are little laboratories.

Burned in His Memory

The slit in her well-traveled sarong,
offers a brief escape for her willowy thighs.

Bridling slightly pigeon-toed feet,
mercurial sandals engage ankles into godlike harmony.

Her back and neck shore up festive tributaries of
bountiful hair.

Elbows that slant in above the hips,
find precise harbor where women moor babies.

Like arrows in a quiver,
a book, flute, and mango, nestle assuredly
in her ethnic shoulder bag.

Saddling on her opposite shoulder mounts a low-slung beach chair,
arming her with the morning mission.

Sauntering across her childhood beachfronts . . .
memories of her father, beckons a smile.
Simultaneously an ocean breeze tips her brimmed hat back;
the childlike face her father held so dear harkens back.

"It" Is Still There

Imagination is being in, "it."
Children live in, "it."
We've grown out of, "it."
But can still identify, "it."
Sometimes we deny, "it."
For granted we took, "it."
Now that we know what, "it," isn't, we miss "it."

The Missing Link?

When Adam and Eve left the garden:
Did the animals feel sorry for them,
or think humans were overly ambitious?

Were they jealous?
Did they fear them,
or even feel a bit suspicious?

Or was the apple story
just too delicious?

Inner Dialogues' Recess

Ego's chatter is the white noise of rain,
constantly drowning the blissful quietude of nothingness.

Real life events seamlessly activate the off switch
(interrupting its reign).

Tolerating reality's interferences,
the interloping dialogue will always return;
then employ it as fodder for future fantasies.

Poetic Tickets

Poetic melodies are spoken. Word.
The line break, dance accents
tension, and relief.

Confessing.
Blessing.
Obsessing.
Shaking the dice of muses,
gambling with vulnerability.

Navigating past depots of destinations,
engineering trains of thought,
it arrives at gates of decisions
through stanzas of poetic terminals.

Passengers in life,
need a lift.
So they read a bit,
which welcomes them home.

Clouds

Traversing through daylight,
bobbing with the wind;
clouds bank water from sun's thievery.

These storm sentries mark time's passage,
acting as sponges in a relative changing sky.

They are chameleons,
perching for perspective in kaleidoscope sunsets.

Earth's highest connection to the heavens,
is grounded in their presents.

Get Out of Jail Free Card

Self-inflicted victimization from poetic self-doubt is killing me.
No need for wolfsbane,
a silver bullet,
or a wooden stake.

Come muses.
Come mentors. Please!

Release me from discontent.
Free me to revel in my creations.

I yearn for the Matrix pill of poetic magic
(doing the work notwithstanding).

Pelican Bobbers

Like bobbers, pelicans relentlessly attempt
to penetrate the water's surface.
Physics greatly inhibits submerging.

They feast on modest fish,
whose only fault is reveling
in the warmth of the surface.

Water's depth shelters larger species,
from plump predatorial pelicans.

Head butting from aquatic pounding,
constantly reminds them of their biological confines;
they poise buoyantly for a genetic mutation.

Future generations of subsurface fish, beware!

Covert Smuggler

She wears large sweatshirts,
smuggling the ordinance of her bra in.

Only after adhering to the appropriate protocol,
will they be prompted, exposed, and jettisoned
from the nestled security of their silos.

Security demands they be handled
with the highest level of sensitivity.

Cloud Wars

Since the Big Bang
clouds march endlessly
in their crusade to overtake enemy weather systems;
escalating a planetary Rock, Paper, Scissors game.

Mars thunderously recruits warlike winds.
Creating funnel clouds of nuclear proportions;
undeterred by collateral damage.

Gloating over victories like Roman emperors,
Stratus, Cirrus, and Supercilious clouds
take turns on Earth's throne/veiling blue skies.

Transient armies of clouds always exhaust themselves.
Consequently a cat game of Tic-Tac-Toe ensues,
then renews.

How We Got Here

Is all this bad news a
curse?
A Sodom and Gomorrah
verse?
Do you think it will get
worse?

Quicker technology means
more news.
Misinformation is such
a ruse.
Confusion doesn't help
our views.

If this trend is accepted
as much,
I get overwhelmed from
lack of trust.
Is this a self-fulfilling prophecy,
as such?

Travelers

Travelers are transient recording devices,
voyeuristically filing sweet memories,
betrothed in the juices of exotic cultures.

Cameras, phones, deus ex machina are proxies,
recording sentiments.
They are Darwinians,
in the Galapagos of their destinations.

Echoing no regrets,
returning with cultural equanimity,
they impregnate a macro planet.

Staying in Hostels at Seventy

Bedrooms are dining rooms;
living rooms are lobbies.
Bathrooms are courteously private.
Everything is a library.
Lodge etiquette is assumed everywhere.

Daily processes start
while waiting in line to brush teeth.
At the sink, good manners warrant
offering a splash of water for them to get started.

Young female travelers are uninhibited in their
half-baked, half-naked, time-tested sleepwear.

Harnesses that normally manage breasts throughout the day
have been removed.
Loose fitting T-shirts swarm over each gland,
smothering any attempts of escape.

A small percentage of buttocks break loose
from their cotton moorings.
Tiring of being held in place all night,
bits peer out with youthful exuberance.

Crossword Poem

In solving crossword puzzles,
only
one
answer
claims

its dwelling place.

Horizontal

and vertical order,

uses
alphabetical
brick
and mortar.

Poetry's words also fit into spaces,
in the street maps of their places.
From the lighthouse of my imagination,
they find mooring from poetic illumination.

Aborted Sneeze

Quick breaths,
watery eyes,
and shifting mucus,
signal a potential sneeze.

The climatic event of thrusting bacteria out on triggered air,
does not always conclude.

Ceasing to execute,
due to nostrils not adequately encumbered, OR
insufficient sunlight to excite tear ducts
dashes any expectations of a well-intended bodily function.

If not jettisoned,
sniffed and swallowed,
we nonchalantly discard the dead white blood cells into a bandana.
Offering no honor to dignify their sacrifice.

Whirlwind of Art

Cyclonic wind sends orphaned scraps of paper,
on tornadic Tilt-A-Whirl rides.
Chinese silk dancers take their inspiration
from these wispy, weightless dances in air.

The ghosts of deceased mailmen are haunted
by their inability
to sort those random, flighty, unfettered, paper objects.

Two Sleeping Worlds

A home security light awakens,
warns and telegraphs
the numbers it addresses.

Against quietude,
a train rumbles through
the sleeping neighborhood it caresses.

Slumbering residents
block out the rattles,
and the scheduled times it professes.

The cemetery's residents
hear not its eternal chugging,
but repose peacefully, as it blesses.

Welcome Back Features

At conception parental DNA creates new cells.
The soul's essence manifests opportunities of self-expression.

Fertilized eggs are shopping carts,
browsing down ancestral aisles in genetic supermarkets.

The roulette, *Wheel of Fortune*,
heralds the child's characteristics.
A karmic Vanna White presents them.

After birth, families identify their victorious bloodlines;
while mothers count fingers and toes.

WaterMagic

Forgiveness is water;
wearing away depths of deeply entrenched forces.

It is the brook of atonement.
Filling and refilling the vessels that heal our souls.

Streams of strength are divined
from the tributaries of the gods.

Still Life on Hardscrabble Road

Deep, full, sodden air,
penetrating scenes, everywhere.
Luminous skies, summon my eyes . . .
down curious roads where nature hides.

I see plowed, planted, and necklaced rows, anointed
by swallows, martins, and crows. Accenting quaint
old, charming barns,
they represent half-truths, of my mythological yarns.

From my car's detached point of view,
they appear wholly perfect and enchantingly true.
Wherefore . . .
I only deem necessary a day, maybe two,
for visiting the land of green and blue.

Tree of Knowledge

Energy from boundless sunlight,
pumps nutritiously gorged,
zestfully potent water,
through the conduits of tree roots.
Chlorophyll produces growth; while
expressing oxygen to the world.

Human faculties are tree roots,
tentacles of sensory highway.
Absorbing limitless information.
Like photosynthesis,
they are transforming agents,
turning knowledge into wisdom.
Expressing it to the world.

Surrounding Nothing

Meditation is a mist,
between daydreams and thoughts.
The nourishing segue;
drowning ego's chatter.

Invites gentle nothingness
to pause the dutiful dialogue;
and realize the eventless awe . . .
of absolute emptiness.

Time's Hiatus

Soulfully sweeping through time zones,
it neither flies nor slows down.
Desiring only to break its own servitude,
time transcends itself into timelessness.

Meditation, hard work, and play,
are tools for stepping outside ego's precincts.
Cathartic feelings are the only remnants.

Like any cosmic event
it regenerates fertile soil,
and incubates new life.

Tribute to Mose

Parables are allegorical,
paradoxical, and metaphysical.

Ergonomically pragmatic;
but end up catatonically dogmatic.

Ironically existential,
but essentially rudimental.

Appearing simplistically superficial,
in reality are complexly beneficial.

Mr. Bob Zimmerman

I don't need your proselytizing
nor do I want your rationalizing.

I don't need your theorizing
so put away your patronizing.

I don't want to be defined,
condescended to, or realigned.

I don't want to be transfixed,
preached to, denied, or even nixed.

MLK and LANGSTON

I dream of a world where:
Empathy crowns success.
Sharing defines currency.
Greed serves as a protectorate.
Egos take pride in cultural servitude.
Guilt administers to the underprivileged.
Sustainability is our planet's handmaiden.
Hierarchy kneels to equity.

Spring Shows . . . Up

Stealing the dryness of winter,
musty air saturates spring growth.
Prideful arrogance of humble blossoms
declare victory over cyclic sleep.
A confluence of smells,
mesh rich aromas of lilac and lilies.

Soil's abundance replenishes with vigor.
Seeds break through permeable shells, thrusting
into the moist smorgasbord of earth.
Hibernating roots awaken
and engage their breakfast in bed.

Retching Refuse on Teeming Shores

Tides uniformly transport discarded coral.
Acting as torture devices for unsuspecting feet,
we avoid them.

Abandoned and dislocated trees,
dispatched from gorged riverbanks,
lumber themselves to the high tide moorings of accepting coastlines.

Intermingling clusters of plastic refuse,
are vomited ashore by tidal trashmen.
Acting as torture devices for unsuspecting eyes,
we avoid them.

Passing By

At a stoplight.
They . . . in their unkempt attire,

held hands,
glancing tenderly.

He offered her an apple.
Sweet excitement filled the bite. Juices
exploded from her mouth. Willfully,
he mopped up.

The fleeting timelessness of love, gushed
into my memory. Savoring,
what they had given me.

While driving past,
I noticed their sign that read,
"Anything helps."

Relative Humidity

Warm air traps cool air, exposing it as fog.
This strata of quilted batting cloaks the cattails,
and caresses the lowlands.

Camouflaging itself as beauty,
it bestows sovereignty for small mammals from foraging predators.

Outside its veil,
patient raptors wait for the landscaped comforter to depart.

The victorious sun vanquishes fog's laced finery.
Transporting it back to its relatives, the clouds.

Hunting season begins.

Self-reflection

Hurt feelings are beacons for enlightenment.
They plow through the protective roads egos build;
detouring the trust.

Transparency eludes us in the covert land of denial.
Projection is blame's tool, cloaked in the wardrobe of others.

The reflection in the mountain lake projects a clear perspective;
showing our true splendor, with bountiful eyes.

Sleeping Fears

Slumber's uninhibited access to repressed fears,
release symbolic scenarios from the cages of our safety;
spawning tales of fleeting nightmares.

Dawn whisks the cryptic storylines away,
but not before stalling momentarily, like deer,
vanishing into the wilderness of our memories.

Puppy's First River Adventure

Her keen sense of smell,
heralds hidden aromas from musty riverbanks.
Surfacing like clues, her nose leads the investigation
through archaeologically concealed secrets.
She rolls in aromatic riches,
tempting curious dogs to witness her odiferous prestige.

Boats send squads of waves as stampeding river monsters.
As the impending threats march toward her,
she bites at them.
Like candy floss, the imminent threats disappear.

While riding home, nasal blasts marinate any and all scents,
adding frosting to a beautifully baked day.

Her obligatory nap
takes her deep into
"Rapid Leg Movement,"
reenacting her victorious river adventures.

Parenting through the Storm

Children's will is the wind,
tugging on the anchor line.
Each ensuing pull
strengthens the knot of loving convictions.

They may choose to not navigate the recommended course.
Benevolently,
set them adrift.

Avowing their independence,
helps set sail,
in a sea of providence.

Out of the Blue

From the triage of youth, festering wounds are
bandaged over.

Masked in life's battlefields,
relationships detonate latent land mines.

To accept these perpetual beasts,
compassion must escort forgiveness.

Before this catharsis unfolds,
the healing process is temporarily cursed,
because people blame everybody else at first.

Gauntlet

Silently and unnervingly,
the train of change beckons us,
with no adherence to sensibility.

Shrouded awe-filled journeys
depart with anxious hope,
and soothe expectations with resolve.

The abyss is daunting.
The providence hidden,
the adjustment . . .
divine.

.

Fawn's First Snowfall

Pine bow's outstretched limbs
carry snowfall's weight with umbrella arms.

Branch avalanches from noonday's sun,
strip the shawl from the pine tree's gown.

Mantles of disrobed crinoline
cloak the ground,
surrounding the pine's perimeter.

Sno-cone confectionaries quench the thirst,
of the curious fawn's delight.

Even Steven

It steals water from our pores,
then Robin Hoods them away.
Borrowing payloads from the ocean,
it makes the clouds repay.

Animals and plants, haven't a choice;
they are ambulatory membranes,
regulating without a voice.

We are the metaphor,
a parable for sacrifice and gain.
Victims in our need to transpire, evolving
just to maintain.

Navigating through Life

When goals demand sailing into the wind,
tacking back and forth is necessary.

Logging the switchback trails with foamy blue memories,
dissolves seamlessly into life's liquid canvas.

Expectations on arrival time,
are the only factors that slow us down.

My Companion

Reading by the fire, I smile welcomingly.
She comes into the den, satifised, head hung with tiredness.
A winter's day outdoors with the children has concluded.
She, and the children, humbly surrender to our creature comforts.

In the warm glow, cuddling
on the couch,
she gently kisses my cheek.
She shares winter's imprint with her cold nose.

Her participation with the children astounds me.
She truly is my best friend,
and the best dog I've ever owned.

Still Quiet Soft Out

Plump snowflakes flutter through streetlights. Stealing
light, intended for the ground.
They fashion cone shape silhouettes;
creating Christmas tree holograms.

Fat, flowery, flakes float into
the stillness of calm.

Parachuting down,
night fairies ride them,
through weightless currents of air.

They land tenderly,
like mother kisses,
on the tummies of babies.

Puffy snow perches on fence posts,
creating pearly elf caps.

The rails act,
as a cooling rack,
hosting frosty white loaves.

Anti-ant

For their home and the protection of their eggs,
carpenter ants instinctively search for warmth in the bowels
of our homesteads.

To our, and their, dismay,
they unwittingly post their pathways on our porches,
decks, and basements.

We apply the "magic anti-ant powder," liberally.
Walking on it tricks them into thinking that eating the wood
is the cause of their deaths skyrocketing.

Realistically we don't care about their bewilderment;
we just want them to stop eating our houses.

A Muse Sings

A friend claims drinking and smoking pot,
makes him more creative.
I wondered, "Is it like the windchill factor,
or is it like the bend in the canyon walls,
which actually quickens its pace?"

Muses selfishly implore us to
do their bidding, mine their messages,
unearth their inspiration, and excavate veined verbiage.

They don't really care about our mental health,
only for our longevity.
If, for no other reason than, not wanting to,
"break somebody new in."

Muses prefer their "couriers," to replace their habits with
something cleaner,
like maybe the obsession of always rewriting everything.

Weather's Superstructure

Atmospheric forces, containing
various states of water, collide
and produce weather.

Air is pressured into
adherence, delegating
this limited resource.

Rain bequeaths the dynamic factor in growth and decay, while
blessings of snow protect and insulate.

Like lightning heralding thunder,
the wind trumpets storm's arrival.
Animals telegraph their news on it; fires fuse it,
while hitchhiking seeds and sailors use it.

Without wind's dissonance,
there'd be no word for weather.

Good Grief

Transforming us into emotional chameleons,
feelings are not bashful when grief precedes them.

While augmenting a pinwheel of maladjusted feelings,
its stay is capricious.
Playing hide-and-seek/secretly desiring to be found.

The tornadic winds are willful, and unfamiliar.
Revealing themselves in the safe basements of our
foundations.

Exposing the soil of our dormant souls,
it unearths the musky odors of growth.

Good grief.

A Cold Is Threatening

A catlike influenza bug,
ceaselessly cries at my doorstep.
Guttural feline flirtations plead to be let in.

Threatening the portico of health,
it longs to pounce on my action figure lifestyle,
giving way to latent couch potato existences.

Cathartic idleness,
copious amounts of echinacea
and napping quotients,
act as ammunition in defense.

Untold Scenes

Stands of ash and elm act as ushers,
escorting orchestrated breezes
through branches of theatrical archways.

Neighborhood street theaters offer their youth
as playwrights,
for cathartic self-expression.

Duty-bound mothers, and battlefield boys
recreate archetypal heroes;
securing happy endings.

Young animals also play; kindling safeguards
within their species.

No audiences will witness these plays.
Although throughout all production,
nature sighs a supportive breeze.
Producing the thunderous quietude
of a million leaves clapping.

Alphabet Soup of Intent

A dam of words,
grooms unabridged sentences at the floodgates.
They marry,
spill over,
and infect the shores of consequence.

Words can attempt dishonest charades;
but telltale facial expressions
unveil betrayal
that is unearthed by lie detector eyes.

Two Clear Influences

We cannot see wind,
only its entourage.
Like scorned lovers,
they follow longingly,
in abject pursuit.

We cannot see light,
only its telltale disciples, shadowing its presence.
Wind and light, act as harbingers,
foretelling the faithful followers.
As does the dawn preceding the sunrise.

Light's color spectrum,
reflects back what it cannot absorb.
Paradoxically, we name it that color.

Unlike a canyon's echo that dutifully duplicates,
light does not yodel back
bouquets of color the sun sent to it.

Putting Our Spin on It.

In establishing the longitudinal grid,
our clocks tick in degrees in accordance with Earth's rotation.
(From the sun's perspective of course.)
Not considering the eight minutes twenty seconds it takes to get
here.

The sweeping second hands represents days,
the minute hands announce months,
and the hour hands wobble seasons in.

But workforce bullies harness time establishing limits in their favor.
While saddling the planet's autonomy,
they spirit away personal latitude.

Although time still disguises events as memories,
longing to boomerang them back as lessons.

On Earth As It Is In Us

Clouds direct shadows through orbital pastures.
Tides, like undulating breathing, rise and fall.

Earth's tilting rotations create cyclic patterns.
Endings produce illusions of finality.
Beginnings have homecomings.

Our Sisyphus inner struggle,
pushes the rock of righteousness and forgiveness
toward endless resolve.
The reaffirming wonderment . . . and gravity,
keep me from jumping off.

About the Author

Tom E. Jandric was born and raised in St. Paul and managed to have lots of fun while still getting some things done.

After attempts at careers too numerous to mention, he settled into the film and video business before eventually retiring from the solar industry. He used to make art with light, then he made electricity with it.

He has traveled and written since the foyer of the '70s. As he entered the foyer of *his* seventies, he picked it right up again, like riding a bike. For Jandric, traveling has been an opportunity to ponder and write while still offering a segue from one life transition to another. Writers travel and travelers write.

Jandric has been published in *The Sun Magazine* and reads out loud at local gatherings.

Printed in the USA
CPSIA information can be obtained
at www.ICGtesting.com
JSHW020142261123
52630JS00003B/135

"Tom E. Jandric has delivered a distinctive and insightful reflection of life and living, filtered through a mature artist's keen and curious mind. His poems reveal the work of a compassionate observer gifted with a nuanced and inspired perspective."

—TD Mischke, writer, musician, podcaster, and former radio talk show host

"Tom E. Jandric's refreshing poetry collection engages and entertains with clever, creative wordplay, vivid imagery, and whimsical yet profound observations on everyday life. The poems navigate through relatable topics ranging from the quizzical to the amusing, including grief, parenting, and the common cold. In 'Poetic Tickets,' Jandric writes, 'Passengers in life, need a lift. So they read a bit, which welcomes them home.' These upbeat poems will do the same for any reader."

—Brenda Owens, senior managing editor, national language arts textbook program

"Tom E. Jandric uses precise metaphors and beautiful earthy imagery to make his poetry stand firm. A delightful read."

—Cecil Wade, farmer, poet, and winner of the McKnight Award

LEGACY POND PRESS

$12.95

ISBN 978-1-64343-593-0

51295

9 781643 435930

$12.95

KEITRA M. ROBINSON, J.D.

Life

Re-imagined

From Frustrated to Fulfilled

Autographed
Copy